GREAT ART ATTACK STUFF

with Neil Buchanan

LONDON, NEW YORK, MELBOURNE,
MUNICH and DELHI

Designer Jacqueline Gooden
Editor Penelope York
Senior Art Editor Rebecca Johns
Senior Editor Fiona Robertson

Prop Maker Jim Copley
Photographer Steve Gorton

Managing Art Editor Rachael Foster
Managing Editor Mary Ling
Production Lisa Moss
DTP Designer Almudena Díaz

This edition published in 2010
First published in Great Britain in 1999 by
Dorling Kindersley Limited
80 Strand, London WC2R 0RL
2 4 6 8 10 9 7 5 3 1

A CIP catalogue record for this book
is available from the British Library.

ISBN: 978-1-4053-6118-7

Colour reproduction by GRB Editrice S.r.1., Verona, Italy
Printed and bound by Toppan Printing, China

Dorling Kindersley would like to thank everyone at
Media Merchants for their help and enthusiasm.

Additional thanks to Gill Cooling for editorial help, Piers Tilbury for
jacket design and Gary Ombler for additional photography.

Discover more at
www.dk.com

CONTENTS

CONTENTS

★ *Remember to get permission before you start any of the projects in Art Attack Great Stuff.*

INTRODUCTION

Hi! It's great to be back with Art Attack Great Stuff – another collection of ideas that are easy to make, look great, and have wonderful uses! This book is not only filled with fantastic 3-D models and top decorations – you can also learn how to create really fabulous pictures using some amazing techniques! Have fun and remember that you don't have to be good at art to create amazing Art Attacks! Try them yourself – collect some bits and pieces, grab your pencils and paints, and have an Art Attack!

Neil Buchanan

Tracing paper

Kitchen foil

Tissue paper

String

Kitchen paper

Coloured chalks

Paintbrushes

Split pins

Glue mixture
You will need to make this special glue mixture for many of the projects in the book. Use twice as much PVA glue as water to make a really strong mixture.

Two parts PVA glue + One part water = Finished glue mixture

Gold and silver marker pens

Marker pens ★

Cardboard

Coloured card

Newspaper

Balloons

Poster paint

Acrylic paints

Art Attack bin
Keep an eye on all the bits and pieces that your family leave lying around. Old wrapping paper and boxes may be just what you're after!

Coloured pencils

Clingwrap

Wrapping paper

Geometry set

Hints and tips
Look out for The Head on the pages of this book. He appears throughout, giving you advice, hints, and tips for your projects.

WACKY WATCH

Are you always forgetting what day of the month it is? This big watch calendar could be the answer – not to tell you the time, but the date!

From card to calendar

Materials

Corrugated cardboard Newspaper Cereal box card

Sticky tape Plastic cup Paint

Toilet paper Split pin Small plate

Modelling clay

Scissors Glue mixture

Ruler

Pencil

Paintbrush

Marker pen

Place a ball of modelling clay behind the card to push your pencil into.

1 Using the side from a cardboard box, draw around a small plate onto the card. Accurately mark the centre of the circle using a ruler.

2 Cut the circle out and make a hole in the centre by pushing a pencil through the point you've marked. This is your big watch face.

Make sure you roll the newspaper up tightly.

Scrunch up a small ball of newspaper and place it on the side of the watch as a winder.

Roll up a small piece of paper and lay it across the middle of the loop to form the pin. Tape it into place.

5 Turn the watch over and give it a chunky, 3-D effect using newspaper. Roll up a sausage of newspaper and give it a twist to keep it in place. Wrap it around the outside of the watch face and tape it into place.

6 To make the buckle, take a smaller piece of newspaper and roll it up into a sausage shape. Bend the scrunched-up paper into a C-shape and tape it to the straight end of the watchstrap in a loop.

Make the end of one of the cardboard pieces pointed, just like a real watchstrap.

Use lots of strong sticky tape to stick down the straps.

Draw the shape of your watchstrap onto the card in pencil.

3 For the watchstrap cut the front and back off a cereal box and place them either side of the watch face. Draw a watchstrap that is slightly narrower than the watch face. Cut out the two parts of the strap.

4 Overlap the straps onto the edge of the cut-out cardboard circle and fix them into place. This will form the back of your watch, so make sure that the straps are securely fixed.

Cover the front and back of the watch. It's a good idea to let one side dry before doing the other side.

You may need to pierce the hole in the centre again.

7 To make your basic watch shape really strong, cover it with the glue mixture and then stick toilet paper onto the pasted areas. Leave to dry overnight and the glue will turn hard and strong.

8 Use acrylic or poster paint to decorate your watch. Paint the face white and the strap a bright colour to make it look like plastic. Paint the metal parts gold so that they look really smart.

COOL CALENDAR

A few finishing touches and your calendar will be ready to use. Put it where you can see it easily and you'll never be stuck for the date again!

The big hand must be long enough to reach the numbers on the outside of the face.

The small hand should reach the small numbers.

Helping hand

Watch that you don't make the hands too long, you don't want to cover the dates up completely!

Try out your own strap designs, such as these brightly coloured polka dots.

Making the clock hands

Cut out two stiff cardboard hands and pierce a hole in the end of each one. Fix them to the middle of the watch face using a split pin. Open out the pin behind the watch.

The big numbers represent each month of the year.

When you are happy with the position of all the numbers, go over them in black marker pen.

Paint the watch hands to match the rest of the watch.

Paint the strap any colour and pattern you like. Finish it off by adding details, such as stitching, in black marker pen.

You can alter the date of any day of the year by moving the large hand to one of the 12 large numbers (the months), and the small hand to one of the 31 small numbers (the days).

Dotty dates
Try experimenting with lots of different colours and patterns for your calendar. You could even make a separate calendar for each of the main rooms in your house, so you always know the date!

Finishing your calendar
Once you've painted your big watch calendar, you can add lots of extra details to make it truly unique and ensure that none of your friends will have anything like it!

Draw around a plastic cup in the middle of the watch face to create a circle for the days.

Number crunching
When drawing the big numbers, start with the 12, 3, 6, and 9, and then neatly fill in the other numbers.

Bend the watchstrap backwards so you can stand it up on a tabletop.

Numbering the clock face
Your watch face has two circles with numbers on: 1–12 for the months and 1–31 for the days. The numbers should be evenly spaced. For the days, divide up the circle into 31 equally spaced sections.

JUNGLE FRAME

Have you got a picture or a photo that you'd like to frame in an unusual way? Why not give it a safari feel with one of these frames?

Materials

Newspaper and picture

2 long and 2 short sticks

Kitchen roll   Glue mixture

String

Glue stick   Modelling clay   Paint

Scissors

Paintbrush

Pencil

Marker pen

From sticks to frame

Make the frame twice the height and width of your picture.

Tie the loose ends together and trim them neatly.

1 Take four chunky sticks and arrange them into a rectangular frame. Make sure that the sticks overlap each other in each of the four corners.

2 Cut a long piece of coarse string for each corner and use it to tie the sticks together. Wrap the string three times in one direction and then three times in the other.

The kitchen roll will create a ragged effect.

Paste on lots of layers to make it really thick.

Both sides can be used to display a picture, so don't forget to paint the back, too!

What a mess!
Make sure you lay lots of newspaper down on your surface before you start pasting on the kitchen roll, it can be a messy business!

3 To make the crinkled leather backing, tear a piece of newspaper to fit in the frame. Paste the newspaper with the glue mixture and then cover it with lots of squares of kitchen roll.

4 Leave the glue to dry overnight into a stiff, crinkled "leather" effect. Use a tan-coloured poster or acrylic paint to paint both sides of the backing.

Make sure each piece of string is long enough to reach the frame.

Use just a little glue around the edges of your picture.

5 Place a ball of modelling clay behind each corner and push a sharp pencil through the paper to make a hole. Thread a piece of string through each hole and then tie the string to each corner of the frame. Use the same string as you used to bind the corners.

6 Choose a picture or a photograph that will fit inside your frame. You may want to stick to the safari theme and find a picture of a fierce animal! Cut it out, put a few dabs of glue on the back, and position it in the middle.

Jungle safari frame

If you tie some string to the top stick, you can put your frame wherever you like – on a door handle, on a shelf, or even above your bed!

Draw on extra details, such as footprints with a black marker pen.

You can make your frame any size you like, depending on what you want to go in it.

Keep out!
If you haven't got a picture or a photo that you want to frame, why not make a safari sign for your bedroom?

WIGGLY EARS

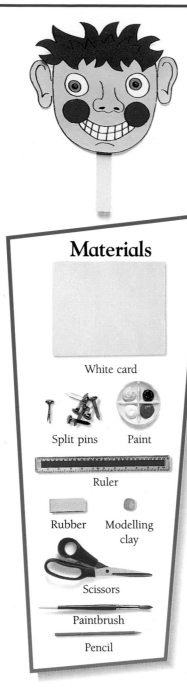

Try this cheeky idea for size – a face with ears that wiggle, thanks to some card and some split pins!

From card to face

Place a lump of modelling clay behind the strip and make a hole by pushing a pencil point into it.

Materials

White card

Split pins   Paint

Ruler

Rubber   Modelling clay

Scissors

Paintbrush

Pencil

1 On a piece of card, draw around a 30-cm ruler twice. Draw an ear shape at each end of one of the strips. Cut out both strips, and cut the ear strip in half.

2 Pierce a hole 2 cm in from the end of the long strip, using modelling clay, as above. Make a hole at the ends of both ear strips, also 2 cm in.

Mark a point midway between each ear and the split pin and make a hole through the marks.

These holes will be the eyes on your face. You will eventually attach your wiggly ears to the face through these holes.

3 Overlap the three pieces of card and join them together with a split pin. Fold back the edges of the pin to secure it. This is your wiggling ear mechanism.

4 Take another piece of thin card and place the wiggling ear mechanism on top. Mark on the card the position of the inside edges of the ears and the halfway holes on the ear strips.

Walter Wiggle Ears

When you have finished painting your face, cut it out. Place it on top of your wiggly ear mechanism and attach them together with split pins through the eyes, splitting the pin at the back. Turn Walter over and give him a good old wiggle!

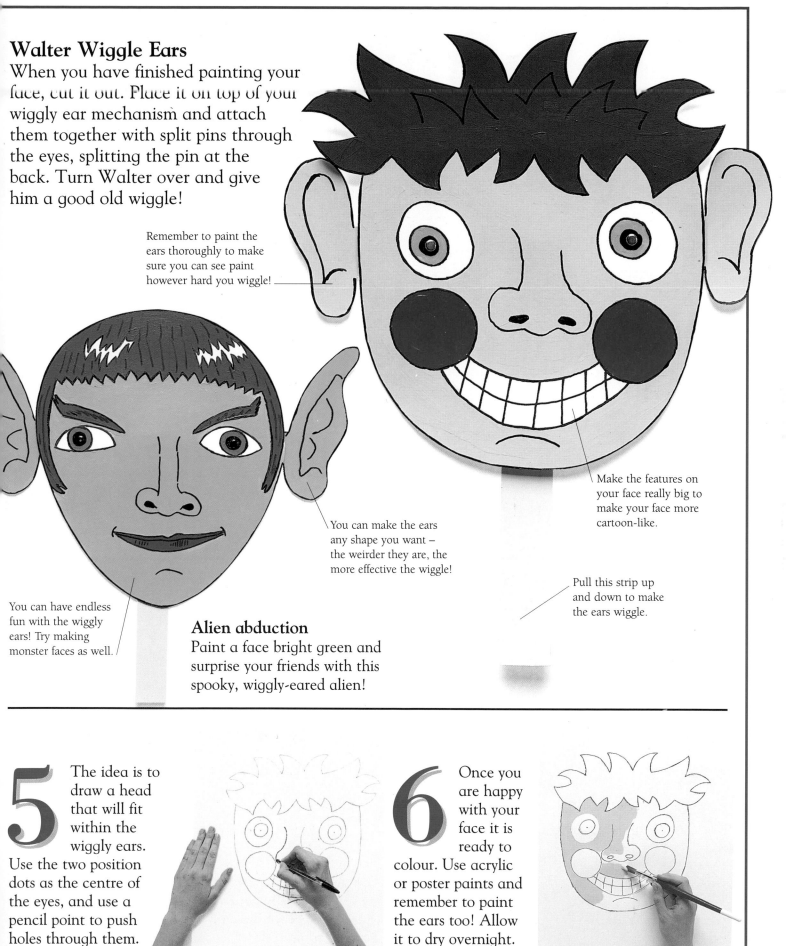

Remember to paint the ears thoroughly to make sure you can see paint however hard you wiggle!

You can make the ears any shape you want – the weirder they are, the more effective the wiggle!

You can have endless fun with the wiggly ears! Try making monster faces as well.

Make the features on your face really big to make your face more cartoon-like.

Pull this strip up and down to make the ears wiggle.

Alien abduction
Paint a face bright green and surprise your friends with this spooky, wiggly-eared alien!

5 The idea is to draw a head that will fit within the wiggly ears. Use the two position dots as the centre of the eyes, and use a pencil point to push holes through them.

6 Once you are happy with your face it is ready to colour. Use acrylic or poster paints and remember to paint the ears too! Allow it to dry overnight.

WRITE AWAY

Personalized stationery can be expensive, so why not have some fun printing your own original designs – using your hands and feet!

From paper to personal stationery

Materials

Cardboard and A4 white paper

Paint   White envelopes

Messy Business!
Make sure you ask permission before you start. It's great fun but can be very messy! Try printing outside.

1 Place a piece of paper on newspaper. Dip your foot into some poster paint, and then press your foot on to the paper.

2 Experiment with the patterns you make on the paper. Try dipping your foot into lots of different coloured paint.

Cut shaped templates out of cardboard.

Put a couple of thumb prints on the envelope too, for an unusual effect.

3 Make some envelopes to match your writing paper! Follow the instructions above, but this time dip your hand in the paint, then press all or part of it firmly on the envelope.

4 You can also use cardboard templates to decorate your stationery.
Dip the template into some paint and press it down on to the paper or envelope for a nice textured finish.

Orchard Cottage
Little Hampton
Gloucestershire
GL8 2PY

1 April 1999

Dear Grandma and Grandpa

I hope you are well. I had a lovely time in Cornwall last weekend. The weather was very sunny and we spent lots of time playing on the beach. I built the biggest sandcastle of all!

The sea was very cold but we still swam all day. Jack has learnt to swim but he still has to wear arm bands when the waves are big.

Lots of love,

Emma

Put your foot in it!

Now that you have decorated your paper, you are ready to sit down and write some letters! You could write to a relative, perhaps, to tell them about your weekend. Or maybe a close friend has moved and you want to catch up with their news.

For a more interesting pattern, press only part of your foot on the paper and use lots of different colours.

Mr and Mrs H G Foote
The Gallery House
Art Attack Road
Maidstone
Kent TN20 9JY

Remember to address your letter correctly.

Clean fingers

Place a loop of tape on the back of the cardboard templates. You can use this to pick up a template and dip it in the paint without getting your fingers messy.

Up, up, and away!

Here's a clever idea – why not turn your thumb prints into balloons? Position the balloons on the page, as if they are floating, and draw pieces of string below them.

Decorate the envelopes to match the paper.

COLOUR WISE

Have you ever noticed how some colours give a warm feeling to your pictures and others give a cool feeling? Try drawing a picture using both.

A winter scene

Materials

Black paper

Coloured chalk

White chalk

Colour swatches

A good way to sort out your colours is to make a colour swatch for each season. Think of the appropriate colours and then draw them all on one sheet of paper as a guide.

This colour swatch has cool colours on the top half and warm colours on the bottom.

1 Draw a picture in warm colours – they are easy to recognize, just think of warm sunshine and hot fires – reds, oranges, yellows, and white. Start your picture, using yellow chalk, by drawing a cosy room with a log fire.

2 Bring some oranges and whites into the picture. The colours will help the fire glow with heat in the grate, and make the room feel cosier. Smudge the fire a little with your finger to spread the heat into the room.

3 To finish the warm colours, add some rich, hot reds. Highlight the fire with small strokes of red and draw in the curtains, chair, and lamp. Can you see how much warmer the room is by using these colours?

4 Finally put in the cool colours – snowy whites, icy blues, and minty greens. Put the colours in the window to make the outside seem snowy and cold. Now you can really see the difference between the warm and cool colours.

Winter warmth

Even though you have used a black background, you still get a strong feeling of warmth just by using the right colours. The icy cool colours and the fiery hot colours really give the picture a cosy, wintery look.

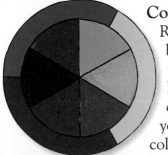

Colour wheel
Red, yellow, and blue are the primary colours. By mixing these colours correctly you can create any colour you want.

The winter colours give a frosty feeling to the outside world.

Autumn days

When you draw an autumn scene, imagine the colours of the falling leaves during this season – rich reds, oranges, and lots of browns. Draw your own autumnal picture using these colours.

Lazy summer

Try out the summer colours and think of strong yellow sunlight, which makes the colours bright and cheerful. Use the primary colours to help the picture seem really sunny.

Spring fever
Spring colours include blossom pinks, daffodil yellows, clear sky-blues, and fresh greens. Draw a picture with these colours and create a crisp, spring feeling.

FANTASY FLYER

The fantastic futuristic fliers in computer games or space movies begin as models. Why not let your imagination run wild and design one yourself

From box to flyer

Draw a line linking the wings together.

1 Take a wedge-shaped box and place it on to a strong piece of card. Draw a large, chunky, triangular wing on either side of the box.

2 Remove the box and draw a line between the wings. Cut out the wings neatly, making them nice and straight. Take a ruler and use it to bend the wings (right).

Cut another toilet roll in to two halves and stick it on the underside of the plane, to match the one on top.

Stick a bottle top onto the cup at the front of the aircraft, and an old ball point pen lid onto this to make the aircraft streamlined.

Stick a sweet tube between the two toilet roll halves on the top of the plane.

5 Cut down the length of a toilet roll and open it out so that you have two half circles, joined in the middle. Stick it to the top of the flyer to make it look hi-tech!

6 Stick sweet tubes and old ballpoint pens under the wings as jet engines and rockets. Put part of an egg box on the top of the plane as the cockpit.

Materials

Cardboard box card

Sweet tubes

Plastic straws

Wedge-shaped box

Sticky tape

Egg box

Paint

PVA glue

Plastic cup

Toilet roll tube

Silver pen

Scissors

Old ballpoint pen

Ruler

Pencil

Paintbrush

Marker pen

Use a ruler to bend the edge of each wing along the line where it will overhang the body of the aircraft.

To form tail jets and a tail, cut a toilet roll in half and stick a triangle of cardboard in-between the two pieces using PVA glue.

Make sure you tape the pieces together well and leave a space at the top of the box.

These main parts make up the basic structure, but to turn it into a fantasy fighter you need lots of cardboard and plastic tubes to stick all over the body.

3 Turn the card over and place the wings over the wedge-shaped box, so that they slope downwards. Use sticky tape to fix them in position.

4 Stick a plastic cup to the front of the box to form the nose, and stick the tail and tail jets to the back. Take your time doing this; use lots of strong tape and be as neat as possible.

Cut a triangle of cardboard and stick it below the tail jets at the back of the plane to form the tail wings.

You can design and paint your plane any way you like, so that it really is your very own fantasy flyer!

7 Cut drinking straws and place them all over the toilet rolls at the tail end of the plane. Make sure all the pieces of the plane are firmly stuck before you begin to paint the flyer.

8 Your plane is now ready to paint. Use a silver pen to colour the jets and windows and acrylic or poster paint for the rest. Add some PVA glue to the poster paint to make it stick to the plastic parts of the plane.

ON A MISSION

Y our flyers are now ready to go into battle! Hang them at different angles so they look as if they're zooming all around the room.

The broad, chunky wings make your flyer look like a jet rather than an ordinary plane.

Rubbish galore!
The more rubbish you use, the better your jet will look. It's simply a case of testing different things to see if they look good on your flyer.

The cardboard tubes look like extra fuel tanks and jets.

Put the rainbow design on the tail end too.

Rainbow warrior
Distinctive details, such as this rainbow edging along the wings, give the flyers their own identities.

Personal logos
Design your own logos for each of the flyers to make them truly unique.

Use acrylic paint on the pens.

Use card to raise the cockpit above the level of the main body.

20

Let battle commence!
Once you've made several flyers, you can send them into battle. Will they fight against each other, or will they unite to fight an unknown alien force?

Allow each layer of paint to dry before adding more.

Demon fighter
Remember that you're the designer and you can paint your flyer any colour you like. The more detail you add, the more it will look as if it's come straight out of the latest sci-fi movie.

Flaming fuel jets
Use red and orange paint inside the jets at the back to create flames.

The fiery flames on this flyer make it look as though it's roaring through the skies.

Don't throw away your old felt-tip pen lids – they look great as a streamlined tip for the flyer's nose!

Draw on extra details with marker pens when you've finished painting.

Boxed in
The wedge-shaped box is the initial shape of the flyer. Just add any old bits and pieces on to it that you choose!

Gold and silver pens give the flyer a great metallic look.

CRAZY COVERS

Are you fascinated by wonderful old books? Why not transform one of your own boring exercise books into an ancient personal diary!

From new book to old diary

Materials

Writing book and cloth

Toilet paper   Glue mixture

Shoe polish   Paint

Pencil

Paintbrush

Marker pen

Add as many layers of toilet paper as it takes to cover the book.

1 Take a plain exercise or hardback writing book and lay strips of toilet paper on the cover. Paint over the strips with the glue mixture. The toilet paper will stick to the book as it soaks up all the glue.

2 Cover the whole of the front and back of your book. It's also a good idea to coat the inside of the cover too, as this will help to stop the book warping outwards as it dries. Leave your book to dry overnight.

Simply press the pulp onto the book and mould it into shape with your fingers.

3 Your book is now ready to decorate. To make it look old, draw fancy hinges on the sides and metal ends with nails at the corners. Let others know it's a private diary by putting a lock and keyhole on it!

4 When your design is done, take some more strips of toilet paper and dip them into the glue mixture. Squeeze out the excess glue and use this pulp to build up your design into a 3-D relief. Leave it to dry overnight.

Use a soft cloth to rub the shoe polish into all the cracks and creases.

Use gold paint to create the metal effect.

5 Your cover is now ready to colour. You can use acrylic or poster paint, or even rub in some brown shoe polish for an "old leather" effect.

6 To finish off, colour the keyhole, hinges, and nails with gold paint. Draw around the edges of them with a black marker pen.

Paint the inside of the keyhole black to make it look real.

Add details such as nail heads for a truly "old" effect.

An ancient record

Your own ancient personal diary is the perfect place to record all your secrets. And the lock and keyhole warn others to stay out!

Use the pulp mixture to highlight some of the features on your cover.

Pretty palette

Try different looks for some of your other books, such as this bold and colourful palette for your sketch pad.

CHALKY FACE

Create your own crazy Art Attack face using a geometry set and some chalk pastels. Use all the shapes in the set for really wacky results!

From chalk to face

Materials

White paper

Rubber

Geometry set   Cotton wool

Coloured chalk

Black chalk

Pencil

Draw around the inside of a protractor for a smaller curve and the outside for a larger curve.

1 Draw around the shapes in a geometry set to create a face. There are lots of different shapes you can make by placing them at different angles.

2 When you're happy with your design, use different coloured chalk or pastels to trace over the lines thickly. Blow off the excess dust.

Use your thumb or finger to smudge the dust towards the centre of each section.

If you prefer, you can use your fingers instead of the cotton wool ball for this stage.

Use as many different colours as you want.

3 Smudge the chalk inwards with your fingertips. Go over the outline again with a pastel in a darker shade. Smudge this line as well to give your picture a dusty, smoky effect.

4 Go over each line with black chalk and lightly smudge it. Then dab a ball of cotton wool onto some of the excess coloured chalk dust, and dab this around the outside edge of the picture.

Funny features

There are lots of different designs for you to try with the geometry shapes. Stick to the shapes only – don't be tempted to cheat! Remember to blow the excess chalk off your picture before you hang it up.

Use the geometry set shapes to exaggerate some of the features on your face, such as the eyes and the chin.

This rabbit's enormous ears were created with a triangle.

Use the outside and inside edges of a protractor for the rabbit's paws.

Use straight lines and sharp edges to give your monster a frightening face.

Make small teeth using the end of a large triangle.

Bewildered bunny

Add to the weirdness of your geometric picture with a wacky choice of colour to finish it off. Have you ever seen a blue and green rabbit with purple paws?

Metric monster

How about using the shapes to create your very own monster? You can make him as evil or as friendly as you like.

Waste not, want not
Keep the excess chalk dust so that you can dab it around the edge of your picture.

TOP T-SHIRTS

Do you have any old, white T-shirts lying around in your drawers? Why not jazz them up with some brilliant do-it-yourself designs?

From plain to patterned

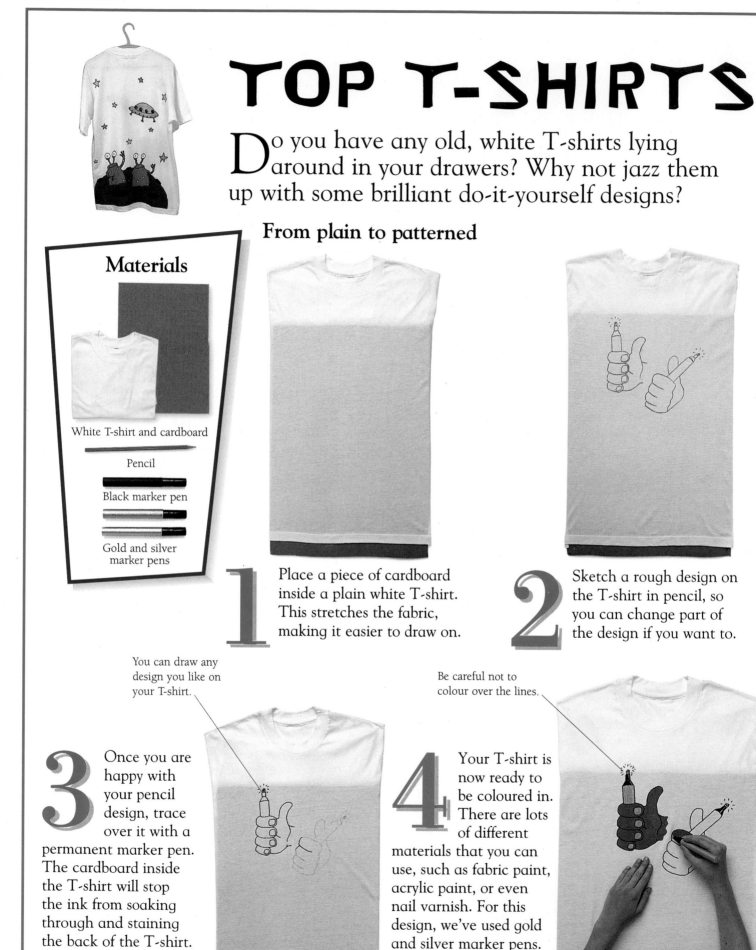

Materials

White T-shirt and cardboard

Pencil

Black marker pen

Gold and silver marker pens

1 Place a piece of cardboard inside a plain white T-shirt. This stretches the fabric, making it easier to draw on.

2 Sketch a rough design on the T-shirt in pencil, so you can change part of the design if you want to.

You can draw any design you like on your T-shirt.

Be careful not to colour over the lines.

3 Once you are happy with your pencil design, trace over it with a permanent marker pen. The cardboard inside the T-shirt will stop the ink from soaking through and staining the back of the T-shirt.

4 Your T-shirt is now ready to be coloured in. There are lots of different materials that you can use, such as fabric paint, acrylic paint, or even nail varnish. For this design, we've used gold and silver marker pens.

Marker pen madness
Marker pens get a thumbs up for a quick and easy way to brighten up a T-shirt!

Make sure you use light, flicked strokes to avoid smearing.

Fabric paints are very brightly coloured and easy to use.

Busy bee
Fabric paints come in brilliant colours and will not fade too quickly. You could even touch up the design with some leftover nail varnish, which is waterproof.

Make sure your designs are big and bold so that they can be seen clearly when you wear the T-shirt.

Paint a special T-shirt for a friend's birthday with a personal design on it.

When the paint is dry, try designing an alien picture on the back too.

Lost in space
This design is perfect for a young space enthusiast! If you paint it with acrylic paints, remember to iron the T-shirt inside out when you have finished, to fix the colour.

Washing care
Always wash your T-shirt in a gentle wash so that the colours stay bright. Materials such as poster paints and felt-tip pens are likely to fade.

27

NEAR AND FAR

Have you ever noticed how things look fainter the further away they get? It's a good tip to remember when you're creating pictures.

From card to mountain scene

1 Cut some rugged mountain shapes out of a sheet of black card. The mountain peaks should be near the top of the page. This will make them look larger in the finished picture. Place the card on a light background.

2 Take a piece of tracing paper and cut it to the same size as the card. Lay it on top of your mountain scene, making sure the black sheet is completely covered. You will notice that the mountain shapes have now faded.

Materials

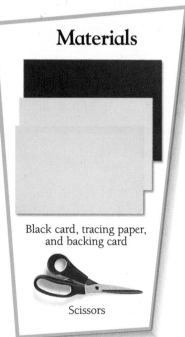

Black card, tracing paper, and backing card

Scissors

3 Cut some tree shapes out of black card. Put the card on top of the tracing paper. The mountains will now seem further away and the trees closer. The layers will give your picture a feeling of depth.

4 Place another sheet of tracing paper on top of the tree shapes. Cut out the shape of a house on a hill. When you put the new card on top you will have three layers of depth and the mountains will seem even further away.

 Layer tip
Start by cutting the background scene at the top of the first card, and as you build up your layers cut further down the card each time. This will ensure that the first layers will seem further away in the distance.

Distant landscape

Place another piece of tracing paper on top. Draw a gate and a wall on a piece of card, cut it out, and place it on your picture as the top layer. The mountain range is far away in the distance, and you have created perspective. Look over the gate and see for miles and miles!

— To give your picture more depth, why not add even more layers of scenery?

Remember to let each stage dry before you begin a new layer.

Remote wilderness

Another brilliant way to create perspective is to paint a watered-down layered picture. For the first layer, mix together a lot of water and not much paint to create the idea of distance. When this layer is dry, paint the next stage using less water for a darker effect. Let the picture dry again, then paint the foreground even darker. Finally use the undiluted paint to draw in finer details. When it is dry, stand back and look into the distance!

The further away the moutains are, the paler they appear.

Draw the nearer balloon lower than the distant one.

Paint the ground nearest to you a darker colour.

Desert highway

The further away objects are, the smaller they appear. Paint a road using this tip. It will be very wide in the foreground and will get thinner as it travels into the distance. Add telegraph poles and a fence, which will also get smaller and closer together. Draw two balloons of different sizes, the bigger balloon will seem nearer. When you have finished, gaze down the never-ending highway!

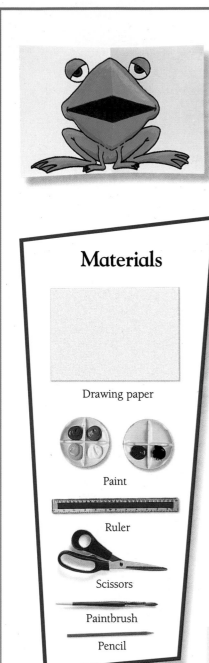

POP-UP CARD

A ll your friends will love this pop-up novelty
card! It's easy to make and much more fun
to receive than an ordinary card.

From paper to pop-up card

Materials

Drawing paper

Paint

Ruler

Scissors

Paintbrush

Pencil

1 Take a sheet of drawing
paper and fold it in half one
way, matching up the edges
of the paper. Then fold it
in half again, matching the
left and right sides together so that
it looks like a greetings card.

2 With a pencil, draw a line
down the fold on the inside
of the card. You will use
this line later to remind
you which part is the inside
of your card. Remember to rub it out
before you paint the card!

Use a ruler to
measure the line
that you will cut.

3 Make sure the pencil line is still
on the inside of the fold. Measure
a quarter of the way along the
folded edge of the paper and mark
it. Cut a straight line upwards
from this mark, half way to the top.

4 Fold back the paper into
triangle flaps, made by the
cut. Crease them well along
the edges. Unfold the flaps,
turn the card over, and press
in the same crease on the reverse side.

As the card starts to close, press down really hard on top of it, trapping the flaps open.

Draw the mouth first, then design the body around it.

5 Open out the sheet of paper. Fold the paper in half along your pencil line crease, making sure the line is on the inside of the card. Put your thumbs inside the slot and pull out the edges of the flaps. Close the card with the flaps open.

6 Open out the card and turn it so that the slot is horizontal, it should close like a mouth. Then draw a simple design on the card, such as a frog.

Friendly fish
Lots of different designs will look great as pop-ups, like this friendly fish.

A ghostly tale
Try making this spooky pop-up ghost for Halloween. Use lots of dark colours for a scary, haunted feel.

Wide-mouth frog
Decide on a background for your picture and then paint it in bright, bold colours. Remember to paint the inside of the mouth, too! You can send your card for a friend's birthday, or even just to say "hello"!

Make the mouth bigger or smaller by changing the length of the line you cut.

PEN PAL

Create your very own pen pal with some paint, modelling clay, and imagination! It looks fantastic, and it holds your favourite pens too!

From clay to pen pal

Make a nose by rolling a pinch of clay between your fingers.

Materials

PVA glue

Paint

Modelling clay

Thin paintbrush

Pencil

Marker pen

1 Roll a piece of modelling clay in the palm of your hand. Make a small, shallow hole in the clay using a pen or a pencil.

2 Push the nose ball into the hole firmly to make sure it stays in place. Use a pencil to make two more holes above the nose for the eyes.

The clay will harden overnight, so make sure you have made all your holes before!

Paint carefully inside the holes so that no clay shows.

Clay tip

Try and find modelling clay that will harden by simply leaving it to dry overnight. You can find it in most toy or hardware shops.

Make the mouth by scratching a line under the nose with a pencil.

3 Mark a mouth with a pencil, then make the pen hole by pushing the pencil in at the side, about 3 cm deep. Twist it a little to open the hole.

4 Leave the pen pal to dry overnight. When it is hard, paint your model with poster paint. Make sure you cover it in paint and leave it to dry.

Perfect pen pal

When the paint is dry, you can cover your pen pal with a coat of PVA glue. The glue looks white and creamy at first, but don't worry – when it dries it becomes smooth, shiny, and rock hard. Your pen pal holder is then ready to hold your favourite pen or pencil. After all, what are pen pals for?

Sink the eyes deep into the head to create a more skull-like look.

Add extra details with black marker pen, such as colouring in the eyes and the mouth.

Make sure your pencils don't clash in the middle when you push them through.

Pink pig holder

The great thing about pen pals is that you can create as many different designs as you want, such as this pig. Try out your own ideas!

Make the ears by pinching some clay into triangles and curling them forwards.

Skull and crosspens!

To create this monster pen pal, shape the clay into a spooky skull and base. Your pencils will look just like crossbones!

To make the pig's tail, roll a piece of clay into a sausage and twist it into shape.

Make sure the holes are deep enough so that the pencils don't topple out!

Handy hedgehog

This hedgehog pen pal will carry a whole range of pens or pencils. The more holes you make, the more pencil prickles you will have! Try using lots of coloured pencils to make the pen holder really stand out.

Pen pal presents

Why not give your pen pals away? You can make lots and lots of pen pal holders from one block of modelling clay. They make perfect presents for your family and friends!

MAGIC MASK

What's a party for unless you can dress up? Here are some wonderful ways to impress your friends and get noticed wherever you go!

Materials

Small cardboard box

Balloon pump

Coloured tissue paper

Balloon

Glue mixture

Modelling clay

Pin

Sticky tape

Scissors

Paintbrush

From balloon to mask

Make sure the balloon is roughly the same size as your own head.

1 Blow up a balloon and place it in a shoebox to keep it stable. The balloon will form the basic shape of your mask.

2 Use modelling clay to make the eyebrows, nose, mouth, and chin. Attach these shapes to the balloon with sticky tape.

Tissue tip
Make sure the tissue paper strips are long enough to create a really interesting border for your mask.

3 Cut long strips of differently coloured tissue paper and stick them over the whole face area using the glue mixture.

4 Build up the balloon with lots of layers of tissue paper. Leave to dry overnight and the tissue paper will turn hard and shiny.

Fabulous faces

Remove the balloon and modelling clay from your mask. Now you have your very own multi-coloured tissue-paper mask to display on your wall!

The eyebrows and other features are raised.

Pop the balloon with a pin, but be careful, it may pop with a loud bang!

Glitter mask

You can decorate your masks in lots of ways. Try sprinkling on glitter and using brightly coloured sequins for a sparkly effect.

Try using layers of colours down the mask to create a stripy look.

Use different coloured glitter for the eyes and mouth.

Pierce the mask with a pencil before you cut out the eyes and mouth.

Stripy mask

Why not cut out holes in the eyes and the mouth so you can wear the mask? Your friends won't recognize you with it on!

FLOWER POWER

Who needs expensive garden centres when you can follow this terrific Art Attack and make some great 3-D flowers!

Materials

Coloured card

Glue stick   Sticky tape

Scissors

Marker pen

From paper to flower

Cut about six more leaf shapes in a bright colour.

Make sure you hold the scissors very carefully when you score lines.

1 Take some green card and draw some flattened S-shape squiggles on it with a pen. Draw a leaf shape around each of the squiggles.

2 Wrap sticky tape around the end of your scissor blades. Carefully, but firmly, score the scissors along the centre line, but don't cut through the card.

The paper will crease easily along the scored line creating a 3-D effect.

Cut a slit from the edge of the circle to the centre, glue along the edge of one of the flaps, and stick it down into a cone shape.

3 Cut the leaves out and crease them along the scored line. Draw a stalk shape and score a line down the middle of it. Cut it out, and crease along the centre line.

4 Make the centre of your flower from a circle of different coloured paper. Lay your stalk down on some backing card and place the cone-shaped centre on the top of the stalk.

Folded paper plant

Experiment using different colours and arrange the petals into different shapes to create unusual flowers. Try making several different kinds and then put them together to create a whole bunch!

The folds give the leaves a really good 3-D effect.

Choose a contrasting colour for your background card.

Draw extra details, such as birds, on your picture with a pen.

Sunny scene

Why not try making other folded paper designs, such as this sunny beach scene? Make important aspects of the picture, such as the sun and the sand dunes, 3-D so that they really stand out from the rest of the picture.

You can make the petals any shape you like.

5 Make some different coloured petals in the same way as the leaves. Making sure you have creased the shapes well, arrange the leaves, petals, stalk, and centre on to the backing card before you stick them down.

Take care not to crush each piece as you stick it down.

6 When you're happy with the arrangement of the pieces, gently stick the shapes on to the backing card. Glue only the sides of each piece. Make sure you keep the 3-D shape by not flattening them.

GLITTER FUN

For this fantastic Art Attack, you paint a picture, not with paint, but with glue. Then you add some glitter for that extra sparkle!

Materials

Coloured paper

Glitter

PVA glue   Rubber   Cotton bud

Pencil

From glue to glitter

Keep the cardboard handy so you can use it on the larger areas.

1 Draw a picture on a piece of paper or card in pencil. Spread some glue over the areas you want to cover with glitter, making sure you don't go over the lines.

2 Use a piece of cardboard to spread the glue over the bigger areas. Try using a cotton bud for the smaller, more fiddly areas.

Create your own pink glitter by mixing gold, silver, and red glitter.

You can make the pink glitter darker by adding more blue glitter.

3 Decide which colours you want to use. While the glue is still wet, sprinkle the coloured glitter over the glued areas. Don't worry about being too neat, just make sure you cover all the glue with glitter.

4 Allow the picture to dry and the glue should soak up all the glitter. Now for the fun part! Simply tip the picture up and shake it until all the excess glitter has come off. Make sure you've covered the area with newspaper first!

Ballroom beauties

Against the dark colour of the background card, the two ballroom dancers look stunning as they sparkle and twirl around the floor.

Turn the lights down low, just like in a real ballroom, and see your picture glow.

For maximum effect use contrasting colours, such as this dark blue and vivid red.

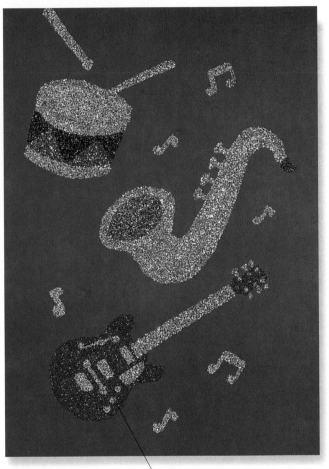

Pick out the detail on the guitar with silver or gold glitter.

All that jazz

What about making a funky musical picture? Draw your favourite instruments and then dot musical notes around the picture for some swinging sparkle!

Exotic parrot

Try making several glitter pictures to brighten up your bedroom walls, such as this exotic parrot perched among the lush green leaves of its tropical rainforest home.

Other bright ideas

Instead of glitter, try using sand or hole-punched confetti to decorate your picture. The results are just as effective!

LIGHT AND DARK

Have you ever tried drawing a dark room? It's simple! All you have to do is let in a tiny bit of light and watch what happens!

From dark to light

Materials

Black paper

White chalk

1 Taking some white chalk and a piece of black paper, begin by letting some light into the bedroom by opening a door. Draw three sides of an open door on the left side of the paper.

2 Now you need to let some light into the room. Use your finger to smudge the chalk away from the door. Try to make your smudges straight as light falls in straight lines.

Shadow tip
Always remember which direction the light is coming from when you draw your pictures. Why not practise by shining a lamp on an object and finding out where the shadows fall?

3 Now there is light in the bedroom, you can see how it falls on the furniture. You can see only one side of the objects so draw the bed by outlining the side nearest the door.

4 Where you have drawn curved shapes, such as the sheets, soften the line by smudging the chalk. Always remember to brush the chalk away from the door, or light source.

Shining light

Draw in some extra furniture to finish off your bedroom and see how effective it can be when you use light and dark. Why not draw your own room? You could even test the light by opening the door in your bedroom a little and looking to see where the light falls.

Make sure you remember to only draw the sides that are nearest the light.

Shadowy street scene

Another way to show light and dark is to add shadows to a picture. The way to find out where shadows fall is to look for the places that light can't get to. On a dark sheet of paper, use chalk to draw a night scene with a lamppost. Follow the light from the lamp and put shadows in the places that don't get any light – down the left side of the man and half way up the wall.

Draw in the light by smudging white chalk on the lamppost.

Make sure you draw the trees smaller the further away they get.

Moonlight silhouettes

Use white chalk to draw a moon and some fluffy cloud edges. Using black chalk, draw in some lines as tree shapes. Shade the edges of the trees that face away from the light. With white chalk, highlight the sides that catch the light. Draw shadows on the ground where the light can't get to. The moon gives an eerie light to the wood.

CREASED ART

Here's a great way of literally making your artwork jump straight off the page – by crunching up paper!

Materials

Wrapping paper, backing card, and coloured paper

Newspaper

Kitchen foil

Glue stick   Glue mixture

Scissors

Paintbrush

Marker pen

From paper to art

1 Take a page of newspaper and draw a person on it. It's a good idea to draw the person in sausage shapes first, to get the right positions.

2 Once you're happy with the body, draw clothes on your person, such as a baseball cap, T-shirt, some shorts, socks, and nice big trainers.

Don't be afraid to crunch up the paper tightly to make them really creased!

3 Cut out all the pieces separately. Use them as templates and draw around them on different coloured paper, such as kitchen foil or wrapping paper. Cut the coloured shapes out.

4 Brush glue mixture onto all the pieces of paper and leave them to dry. When they are dry, they should be hard and shiny. Crunch up each one in your hands to put lots of creases in them.

5 When you have crunched up each piece, practise laying them on to some backing card in their right positions. Piece them all back together like a jigsaw.

6 Stick the pieces down by lightly placing a couple of dabs of glue at the edge of each one. Take care not to flatten them as you do this, or you will spoil the 3-D effect.

In the groove

Try adding other decorations in the background, such as these musical notes in black marker pen, or even some kitchen foil shine for a really funky look.

The musical notes add to the effect of the figure dancing.

Brightly coloured backing board really sets off the main picture.

Soccer star

You can use this technique to create pictures of anything – from a famous sports person, to a pop star, or even your favourite toy!

The creased art effect makes this footballer look as if he's really running after the ball.

Superman's cape billows in the wind as he dashes through the sky on another adventure.

Super hero!

Creasing the paper makes your artwork literally jump off the page! Superman in 3-D!

3-D SCENE

Create an unusual effect by making these amazing see-through pictures. Layer them up and watch how they become 3-D!

From cardboard to 3-D picture

1 Start by making the first see-through picture. Place a piece of A4 paper in the centre of a big piece of cardboard. Carefully draw around the paper with a pencil.

2 Place a ruler against one of the inside edges of the rectangle and draw along it. Do the same along all the edges of the rectangle, so that you end up with a frame shape.

Top heavy
It's a good idea to place some heavy books on top of the cardboard frames as they dry, to really press them together.

5 Apply glue to the other cardboard frame and press the two frames together so that the clingwrap is sandwiched in between. When the glue is dry, trim off the excess clingwrap.

6 While you are waiting for your frame to dry, practise your design on a piece of paper so that you can then correct any mistakes that you may make. For the best effect, keep your picture very simple.

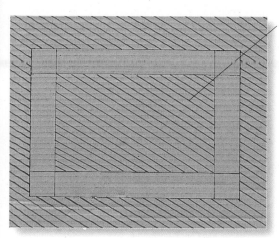

Cut out the red, hatched area by making a hole in the cardboard with a pencil, and then pushing scissors through the hole.

Smooth down the edges with your fingertips.

Take your time with this stage – it is important to roll the clingwrap smoothly.

3 Your frame should be A4 in size and one ruler width thick. Cut it out and then repeat the whole procedure, so that you end up with two frames which are exactly the same size.

4 Apply some glue mixture over the surface of one frame. Stick some clingwrap down on one end and then roll it out to cover the whole frame. Press the clingwrap on to the glue and gently stretch it to smooth out all the wrinkles. The clingwrap should be taut.

Add wispy lines to the frame for a wood-grain effect and paint silver dots to look like screws.

7 Place your picture under the clingwrap frame and trace the design using a permanent marker pen. Just draw the basic shape at this stage, because you can add more detail when you paint it later.

8 Your picture is now ready to be painted. Use either acrylic paint, or poster paint with some washing-up liquid mixed in it to make it stick to the clingwrap. Add little bits of detail to make your picture look realistic.

IN THE FRAME

To make your see-through picture 3-D, simply make three pictures! Lay the frames on top of each other and stand back to admire the effect!

Paint a complete picture on the bottom frame to create a background.

To create a night-time feeling, paint the bottom layer dark with bright yellow lights and a moon.

Clingwrap is very thin, so be careful not to puncture a hole in it as you paint on your pictures.

Outline the details of your picture in black marker pen to help them stand out.

The middle layer of your picture should be only half painted on so that you can see the background behind it.

Night watch

When you have finished painting each picture, place them on top of each other and stand back to admire your amazing 3-D effect! If you stick them together with sticky tack you could even change the pictures around to create a totally different look each time.

Use bright yellow paint to give the effect of a lit streetlamp.

Paint only a few pictures on the top layer so that they will look as if they are in the foreground.

You could design any scene you want. Why not try painting a scene near your home?

A bright picture in the foreground of a night-time scene will really stand out.

Counting sheep
The more cardboard boxes you have, the more frames you can paint. Why not try putting four or five paintings together to create a really big, see-through picture for your wall?

Clingwrap tip
You can draw your picture onto the clingwrap with a ballpoint pen – but be very careful not to puncture the plastic!

INDEX